EDVARD GRIEG

FROM HOLBERG'S TIME
AUS HOLBERGS ZEIT

SUITE IN OLD STYLE
SUITE IM ALTEN STIL

For Piano / Für Klavier

Opus 40

EIGENTUM DES VERLEGERS · ALLE RECHTE VORBEHALTEN
ALL RIGHTS RESERVED

EDITION PETERS
London · Frankfurt/M. · Leipzig · New York

An Frau Erika Lie-Nissen

Aus Holbergs Zeit

Præludium

Edvard Grieg (1843-1907) op. 40

*) Ludwig Holberg (1684-1754) ist der Schöpfer der neueren dänisch-norwegischen Literatur

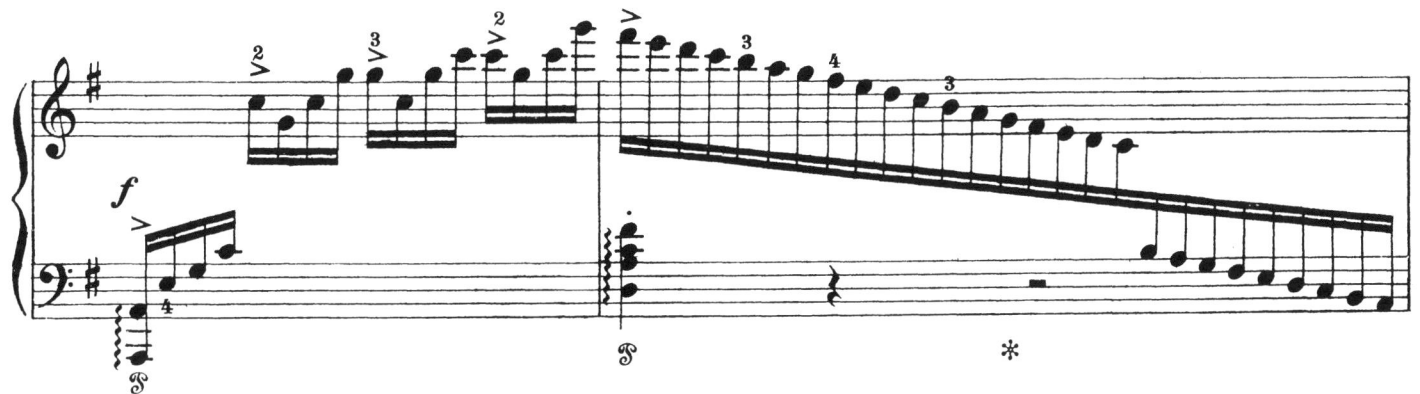

Sarabande

Gavotte

Air

Rigaudon

INHALT

1. PRÆLUDIUM 4
2. SARABANDE 10
3. GAVOTTE 12
4. AIR 14
5. RIGAUDON 18